Swing, Sloth!

Explore the Rainforest

Susan B. Neuman

NATIONAL
GEOGRAPHIC

Washington, D.C.

three-toed sloth

Welcome to the rainforest!

Borneo pygmy elephant

It rains a lot.

There are tall trees.

There is hot sun.

golden bamboo lemur

The rainforest

jaguar

is a good place for animals.

three-toed sloth

Sloths swing.

Snakes slither.

mountain sipo snake

macaws

Macaws cry out.

blue morpho butterfly

Butterflies flutter.

Monkeys climb.

dusky leaf monkeys

Some animals here are big.

gorilla

red-eyed tree frog

Some are small.

Some animals lie on leaves.

Fiji crested iguana

two-toed sloth

Sloths swing in the trees.

The rainforest
is home
to them all.

Rainforest Map

There are rainforests all over the world. Here's where these animals live.

BORNEO PYGMY ELEPHANT
Asia

DUSKY LEAF MONKEY
Asia

FIJI CRESTED IGUANA
Pacific Ocean islands

GOLDEN BAMBOO LEMUR
Africa

GORILLA
Africa

ASIA

EQUATOR

PACIFIC OCEAN

AUSTRALIA

INDIAN OCEAN

EUROPE

AFRICA

ANTARCTICA

NORTH AMERICA

ATLANTIC OCEAN

SOUTH AMERICA

PACIFIC OCEAN

EQUATOR

MAP KEY

tropical rainforest

MACAWS
South America

RED-EYED TREE FROG
North America

TWO-TOED SLOTH
North America

JAGUAR
North and South America

MOUNTAIN SIPO SNAKE
South America

BLUE MORPHO BUTTERFLY
South America

YOUR TURN!

Can you find three animals in the rainforest below?

Book design by David M. Seager

Photo Credits

Cover, Mark Kostich/E+/Getty Images; 1, Michael & Patricia Fogden/Minden Pictures; 2-3, Roy Toft/National Geographic Creative; 4-5, Juan Carlos Munoz/naturepl.com; 6, Banana Pancake/Alamy; 7, Lynn Gail/Lonely Planet Images/Getty Images; 8-9, ZSSD/Minden Pictures; 10-11, Michael & Patricia Fogden/Minden Pictures; 12-13, James Christensen/Foto Natura/Minden Pictures; 14-15, Frans Lanting/National Geographic Creative; 16, Stephen Dalton/Minden Pictures; 17, Elio Della Ferrera/naturepl.com; 18, khd/Shutterstock; 19, Piotr Naskrecki/Minden Pictures; 20, Patricio Robles Gil/Sierra Madre/Minden Pictures; 21, GlobalP/iStockphoto; 22 (frog), Piotr Naskrecki/Minden Pictures; 22 (sloth), GlobalP/iStockphoto; 22 (jaguar), ZSSD/Minden Pictures; 22 (snake), James Christensen/Foto Natura/Minden Pictures; 22 (butterfly), Stephen Dalton/Minden Pictures; 22 (macaw), Frans Lanting/National Geographic Creative; 22 (elephant), Juan Carlos Munoz/naturepl.com; 22 (monkey), Elio Della Ferrera/naturepl.com; 22 (iguana), Patricio Robles Gil/Sierra Madre/Minden Pictures; 22 (lemur), Lynn Gail/Lonely Planet Images/Getty Images; 22 (gorilla), khd/Shutterstock; 23 (frog), Piotr Naskrecki/Minden Pictures; 23 (sloth), Michael & Patricia Fogden/Minden Pictures; 23 (jaguar), ZSSD/Minden Pictures; 23 (rainforest), Martin Shields/Alamy; 24, DLILLC/Corbis; (leaf background, all) Laborant/Shutterstock.

Printed and bound in China by RR Donnelley APS

Did you find them all?